W9-BSN-627

OREXIA

Orexia

POEMS

LISA RUSS SPAAR

A KAREN & MICHAEL BRAZILLER BOOK

PERSEA BOOKS / NEW YORK

Persea Books, Inc.
277 Broadway
New York, NY 10007

Library of Congress Cataloging-in-Publication Data
Names: Spaar, Lisa Russ, author.
Title: Orexia : poems / Lisa Russ Spaar.
Description: First edition. | New York : Persea Books, [2017] |
"A Karen & Michael Braziller book."
Identifiers: LCCN 2016028347 | ISBN 9780892554775
(hardcover : acid-free paper)
Classification: LCC PS3568.U7644 A6 2017 | DDC 811/.54—dc23
LC record available at https://lccn.loc.gov/2016028347 K

First edition
Printed in the United States of America
Designed by Rita Lascaro

CONTENTS

OREXIA

The Wishbone: A Romance

Never to belong again to wings
    that lifted, to heart,
to blood's forsaking bodice:

this lyric forceps,
    felled flèche d'amour,
furcula picked and dried

with earthy feints of sage
    & fused with remnant gristle—
clavicles tongued, now thumbed,

memento mori
    of a hard year. Why not,
then, after giving thanks,

break it, too—
    talismanically? What good
is loss starved forever after?

To keep from freezing,
    even a priest might commit
the Virgin's statue to the flames.

Temple Gaudete

Deus homo factus est
Natura mirante.

Is love the start of a journey back?
If so, back where, & make it holy.

St. Cerulean Warbler, livid blur,
heart on the lam, courses arterial branches,

combing up & down, embolic,
while I, inside, punch down & fold a floe

of dough to make it later rise.
Recorded Medieval voices, polyphonic,

God has become man, to the wonderment
of Nature. Simple to say: there is gash,

then balm. Admit we love the abyss,
our mouths sipping it in one another.

At the feeder now. Back to the cherry, quick,
song's burden, rejoice, rejoice.

O salve & knife. Too simple to say
we begin as mouths, angry swack,

lungs flooded with a blue foreseeing.
Story that can save us only through the body.

Owl Hour

Houseless against gray glower,
juniper dank, grisaille pagoda firs,

& sounding an unplumbed sleeting
within, girlhood's obscure guilt lingering,

a voice calling you inside, this betiding
fur-stirred wedge in high oak, jacketed child,

prehistoric eye in unlikely presiding
above the park's trapeze of empty swings.

I know it will disappear
if I look away. To be clear,

Figment, seed invisible in pent snow:
any mutiny in this going is mine, I know.

Baroque Hour

In which death yields to style:
ruddled vista humping intricacies

of vines, twinings tombed & calligraphic.
Is this distortion possible only in lies,

folds, the enigmatic golden stall
prose gnaws the edges of—

this cedar nave blooded by sundown
suddenly become all my self,

one doomed syllable, like *young*?
Unlike infinity, which has no native tongue?

Crooked Light

I love you, December,
your dusks iodine

as tea that scolds the water.
Your sickle glimpses,

grouted hemlock, hollies,
satin-black at evening,

wincing in mid-day's
cracked, cutlery glare.

I drink your ending,
ice of childhood, pond

thick as my waist but condensed
as seed, secret in a waiting place.

Skating, skating against sadness,
I suckle you, Paradise.

Yearn for me. Bent & bird-ricked,
be a fiction I believe.

Worry Yoga

A sheer pleat of hamstrung distraction,
the heart opens, says the teacher.
Don't push so hard with the eyes—

*let the world see you—*this while touching
my fontanel as a cruciform jet
scores a corset of cloud filling the high window.

In the studio, on whose account
do I recall myself again, scumble
of vexation in a child's pose.

Is it masochistic to *think*
while following the open hand as it traces
lost houses, loves, states of mind?

I know you feel them, too, the holes
slipped into the torso—*sorry, story.*
Palms pressed, I unbend,

follow the vertebral way,
hold an "o" before my ribcage,
space the size of the green stone,

marbled lode from a land of sorrow.
The burr in worry, "r's" like hitchhiker seeds,
arcing lures that bend, twist away,

then float slowly home. Freedom is the first
and our last urge. It breathes us.
I adjust, one needing

such juxtapositions.
At prayer I slipped the cool mineral
between my gown & heart. Stippled.

Remorse

A stick wrapped with sour sponge
to wet the lips; a grave dug

for the sacrificed heart.
Catheter that won't insert.

This lit chain of stores where families eat
beside a highway, wet with rain.

The hurt you feel tonight I made.
It makes me small, crouched again

beneath a desk, spindly, wobbled
open maw that held a ruler,

mess of pencils, books in newsprint.
At the stoplight now, weather unspools

windshield lesions. Someone somewhere
tunes a bomb to her body.

In extremis. What a pain
like hers must feel like, bifold life,

this or that, I can't imagine.
Strapped to mine is yours, I am

extended past our species.
Nuclei in our four hands.

Feet with penitential tongues,
pray here, pray now, always pray for

to be given.

Celibacy 1

Unmarried, the heart ejaculates
what it must, scarlet-purled, arterial,

away, away. Or conversely, married,
it requires all—venous, freighted with waste.

Fuck the heart. On the radio,
driving home, I learn the Brits

are into all things Scandinavian.
Sunlit schools, bare breasts, the Aurora Borealis.

A "scandi trance." Maybe. Ice is a mystery
of whatever blue enchantment swiped

my view this morning. This is no allegory.
I'm north of myself these days

with a fist full of silver keys
I lose every night in my dreams.

Friday Night Hour

Is it spectacle I'm avoiding
in a logic of surrogacy,

pharmakon gauntlet trees,
corrosive golds, birds in flexed design,

lifting, standing in for an evening
gathered with couples

or taking in a film? Bite me,
charred gusts, as I, solo,

open a window to light's shank,
to Venus, lone & salt-stung earring.

The etched in wretched. Sure.
Inward hardly mean no drama.

But it's a different kind of transit:
day's demise that shows us we're alive.

Temple Solstice

Glinty as spittle,
       prink of shortest-day sun
straddles the black ridge,

vault whose ancient pewter speech,
       parsed by cloud-cleaved
pulmonary geese, pulsed leaves,

draws me into ohmming hemlocks,
       saint's sleeves,
vulnerable resinous wrists.

Beyond or suffused with pain?
       Both. Even the moon
does not speak my language

as many times as we've conversed.
       Comb me, tricked-up wind.
Quick, before you change your polar name.

Ice Idyll

Old boxwood cloven overnight by storm,
sharp storax ambar & hoar-caped steam

lingering like that elusive dream,
What was it? That the stolen car or key forgotten

in a murky city is another word for dread?
Boot grunt, chainsaw, panic, stridor

of scarved breathing, what's far sounds near;
what's close, years off. The dream, was it wondering,

Is god the first memory, how die without something
to remember, is there room in the huddled body

for this captured tune? Saturnalian, chandelier
oaks grovel under cloud cudgel. Engines catch, slur.

The lawn strigose. Everything in the register
of clavical, pelvis, shiv & clank noblesse,

silver on bone, on plate, places I cannot guess.
Clear nocks shedding from bamboo beyond the firs.

Glass coffins, brush dense with birds. Saline slurry.
Milk-white, a talon hangs frozen from the concrete bath.

Idolatrous, armored by a sheer, worshipful wrath,
could even winter swear I'm made of words.

Temple Moon

Hazel cameo, clipped nickel,
God's oyster, stone eye of a saint,

host pearled as the clock's pendulum orb
nodding *no, no, no* to sleep, to music

arked in the mahogany kiosk
of faith's metronome. *No,* you say?

Perhaps I should find another muse.
(O tipsy moth, unshroud slow

the musted wools of self!)
Last night, downstairs, unbeknownst,

you dropped your lunar sharp
on a sleeping ivory key. Afraid to die,

I lay upstairs listening to ruin.
I thought rain.

That's my confession, sky wound.
The voweled vow of you, of pain—

Abridged Hour

All metaphor is death? Hmmm.
So the love I bear him

becomes this running scripture
of scarlet creeper, evening's silver pitcher,

abraded sun, clenched hand diving
from ether to earth in under five?

And while we're talking shortcuts,
these are mine: dark when I woke.

Fought to move past actions
of mere perception.

Took a pass on jealousy's old habit.
Drove through fall's theatrics

only to have my self effaced, a proxy terror,
cutting my mother's moon-white hair.

The Saintly Vita

As for hair-shirt vest,
    tomes gut-strung, spinning
from rafters, headless islands,

relic pelvic bones, stone-fruit pits
    erose, grilles, shackles,
hardened excrement, cicada snoods,

each night's bad dream
    a pin-prick planetarium, well
hold it right there. Heresy

means choice. You. Pestle edge
    whiff, making me
wife of eternity,

you—altar—inverting
    o'clock's pendulum.
You endlessly unsolvable sum.

Temple Dictionary

Seeking "tresor," from the Greek
thesaurus, store, treasure house,

I find this filament stem & venous stain,
last spring's violet,

genital lapels held in tiny, kama sutric
kimono foldings, obeisant

to the word "thesis," *a setting down.* Down.
Forgive me, O once-alive.

I believed to press love
would be to make love. See?

You are here again, bruised syllable
that consumes all flesh.

Can a word have soul? How move
from one to the next without dying?

Furta Sacra

I believe in holy theft.
Pelvis bone of St. What's-His-Name

hoisted above famished fields for rain.
Knuckle of the Mother for luck.

Splinter of manger. Shards,
ephemera, wholly haloed.

To hold a relic is to change it,
under glass, with ropes, a ring of stones.

Lord knows to protect love
costs a tender violence.

Head trimmings pressed
between crystal lenticels.

Crescent horn of fingernail in locket;
rogue, lure-hairs, a spell of seed

captured in places unmentionable.
Unadorned, unfigured,

with hands and more we've stolen.
Gut-twisted silver winter. Ghost gold.

Mynddaeg Hour

Mind-day, old word
for the year's turning

over prospect's sable pew,
just words left, then,

time already thinning.
What is not God's day?

But this is ours.
Let's save our souls

for later, in favor
of the body' disguises,

bell-pull spine, fisted hair,
heart's buried watch.

In another kind of tale,
a glass shoe might drift in your hand,

a future, on bent knee.
Unshod desire, instead,

steps out when we're old
in the names of fur, toenails,

wren the nest becomes.
That voltage. How not die?

We will. Fawn felled by the roadside
on the drive home. We're her bride.

Temple You

What is mysterious about loss,
flush of arm pulled from a wilted sleeve,

summer's urine-tang in winter leaves?
Let John Keats light another fag.

Or Brontë refuse the doctor
on her black sateen settee.

For whatever part of you
may be taken away, you said,

is the scar, the place, I will visit first
with my mouth, each time,

as gold visits the thieved till,
sun the obliterated sill,

saying thank you for leaving
me this you, this living still.

Celibacy 2

Nervous, twigs split, become swallows,
jeté the platinum poring chits

over the mountain's bistered tinge.
Is a murderer secreted in each one

of us, someone we once knew,
even embraced in a mirror

without premonition? No way
this season knows it's ending.

Instead of "murderer," let's say "orphan."
You're leaving, you say? Either way,

what to do from here to then,
when language means to stay?

Venus Hour

Enter the mind's sky,
why don't you, at winter's edge,

blooded, the love of wrists
still splitting the west,

you, in love with blue—
force more true

than even my ardor for it—
you new-apparent, emerald instinct

above dormer, rafters
fringed with bangs of lights.

Thong of my song, Love wrote,
summers ago. Scraps of paper,

tablet on the tongue. Calendar pages
flying. Pistil-sting. Sails.

You, caught in the rigging.
Night's prize. You undenied.

Temple Age

Sycamores phrasal, ashen,
strap, bi-chromatic,

this cross-hatched patch of woods.
Respond with hard answers, please.

My season is upon me.
Green in there somewhere, yes,

even red, if I hash around?
Goodbye beauty, I might also say.

Depart loveliness, at last.
Passing by pallid fields,

I confess I dreamed of us.
Precarious weeks, these,

that never want me small.
Or parceled. Rather all.

Snowdrops

for Claudia

Eyesome, still in habit
full-druped & greeny,

as you were, first shouldering,
weeks ago, the very night winter,

pinched, sodden, dropped its overcoat,
sooty chilblains, chins of snow,

& yet this morning, just shy
of equinox, in wake of melting,

you, pagan, drunk on sky's milk,
find me. Temptation of sadness.

Bract, scape, dilator of death's
fisted rooms, you sing

your blue, your worried note.
As though you suffered for me,

kneeling in pine snuff, in brackish
chord of your light, incurable.

Hare

As light fails, despite ceaseless rain,
she comes, for my phlox, cotton lavender,

doused & two-dimensional, apprehending world,
whatever that is to her, in the slight tremor

& pinch of flank, the one eye
rolling in hazel truckle, feral, desolate,

the other wayward, gazing who knows where,
in mated gambol or placid trench of lilies, flares,

or across the lawn's green sea, vitrine lens to you,
traveled afar, under grapevine, above a bowl

of oil & blue heap of scraped shells, reading.
Always the tug between what touches (the wine,

salted lips, fork, tongue, lapped napkin),
& what looks. She's hungry. I want to defend

what I think I've grown. How see each other
except through this knowledge?

The sodden yard, the minute sudden snails:
to see something whole, must we make it small

the beloved a pupil in the eye? This creature
constructs, in the scale of her scribbling heart,

an ancient mind: a private, besieged chamber
that dilates a hair's breadth, you to remember.

Plum Hour

Brought beneath my instep by storm,
orb flung to wet sand path this morning,

you wreathed, sheathed verb,
you hold uncharted, turquoise, filmic,

sugared by treasons, ocean
tissued as the eye of the she-robin

that pelted door-glass yesterday,
then lay, twitching, for hours in my gaze.

Rise, I prayed. *Fly.* Into the naked terroir,
season of desire beneath & so far

inside me I'm already way beyond mind.
Fused, griding there, still upright

as within skin, I believe I—
until words come again. What is dying

if not the told clung stone, self, future
falling through blind flesh, tor,

toward *I died, I still live,*
which is the myth love makes of us.

"A Labour of"

In St. Alban's *Terms of Venery*—murder,
pride, crash, exaltation—

this one is for the earth boars, sows:
blind, droll, clay-licked moles

two-thumbing with sickle paws
the ground beneath me,

frangible with innuendo,
warped by subtext and a double,

simultaneous life of larder, tunnel,
inconsummate infidelity.

I try to walk upright there every day,
nonetheless. Sometimes twist

an ankle, stir yellow-jackets
laired below the stump.

Solitaries all, perhaps.
But I'm not buying that.

Mouths have scoured my buried bulbs.
What eats dirt for no good reason?

Scarlet Tanager

Bated ruby, guru occult,
you show yourself to us

after we—in gambit of breed,
of anchorite, of wind-thieved

bondage—have broken fast
an hour terraced, gifted.

Released from our old names,
no need now to pronounce

yours. Unleashed dogs,
magnolia tongue, galleries of cloud

scud your historical, destined tidings,
votary, from branch to branch.

Where now? Where ever be your twigs
& shell & twining, be our flying.

Temple Surrender

Fingernail-curried bark,
vinegar leavings, dusk's plush,

as in our conversion, bent, braced,
I was subordinate to a dominant

clause already devouring the push-back
prising open of the sky. Do not think

I strayed, or for a moment stopped
tracing with mental tongue

that silk seam that runs—
you see my train, wrists pinned.

Tomb, womb,
let's not forget what we are.

Helpless with you,
inked copse of verge

lifting into undefiled summons
of star-stalked sky.

Bitten moon. Perfect.
What's to come.

Wandering Womb

Inching toward the vagus, maybe?

Chasing its own casino, inland sea

before skidding off, slo-mo,

on retro pinball bumpers, pheromones

blinking, honking, volume low.

Then stalled as the animal

housing her dips a drowsy toe

into an elision post-coi,

sepia, sleep's ruin, grave

where pubic-fine green lawn framed

by granite molars utters lost foundation

still stories high in places pocked with lindens

sprouting out of mortar in airy wisps

the swallows course & rimple.

She is cathedral partial, all nerve,

all limpid ink. Watch her swerve

into thought-balloon, hoisting above them

a decades-long succession of carnal hymns.

Hour Bleu-aille

I'm a magpie, true, but want
also to be possessed.

Twilight's eviscerating interval
that verse makes visible:

if there is nothing to be
ravished in the lineated transfer,

I'm out. You are not me,
which is why I take

your blue seriously. Tamper
rhetorically, any way you like.

Cut my pages. Open my fan,
bamboo couplets, pasted paper wings.

As for the title, I never know
how to pronounce anything.

Orexic Hour

My body, made to be entered
& exited. Almost wrote "edited."

Eaten. Odd to be so direct.
Who cares that the maples blistered

with renewal today, at last,
despite shackles of snow,

not for me, not for you,
obeying an instinct akin to human,

but not. Still freighted
by the gadget of a self, I admit

I care. Is it my appetite for this violent
flux—crocus mons afloat beneath oaks,

stamen odor, bulb-aroused mouth—
that, against effacement, I invent?

Mystic Toys

Balconies of green, unrefrained rain,
steaming, ungirdled in culverts,

whelming gutters, spouts, sun an amnesiac,
erased imprimatur, & what reigns

in this house is the musk of abandoned warrens,
ammoniac carpet spores, dank closets

emitting sweet scarlatina—hem, towel,
infant receiving blanket, the absence

of fat-dewed cheeks, foreheads mouthed
with wishes. None of them

is here, enchanted bodies hefted, fed,
sponged, sung to sleep in a museum

of dolls, whose eyes would fail to close,
later, on their backs in boxes beside the curb,

& looming creatures rubbed to fever sheen,
rooms made wavery by slaked windows,

silvering a shoe left behind, stiletto,
faux leopard, with turquoise sole,

& this remnant—thong—unlikely fret, amethyst
spider floss—hardly daughterly—& yet,

stooping, water recalls palatial ice, the larger
space it took, the weight impossible it held.

Trust Hour

The rust in it.
The hard-wired rigor mortis,
knee-jerk, historical.

You are suspicious,
Heretic, of slack nostalgia.
Denial, jealousy, & such craft.

The instant of "no choice"
occurs, tea-maker says,
when there is just one need:

boil, steep, serve.
Your hand over my heart
shows me shape

of cup. No formula
except suffer, sip, swallow.
Gladden. Drink again.

Temple Serein

Who wouldn't treasure this pain,
cloudless sundown sly with rain,

a slight, houndstooth-tinged hour
almost hormonal. Remember?

Uncanny blue static between child cry
& breast fill? The body made to shed itself.

Between window glass & dank screen
a spider in skeletal ruff with bony pincers

swaths, rolling, rolling with clinical precision,
a hapless gnat in miniscule candy gauze.

No longer girl, I don't *want* to suffer—
finger in flame or door jamb,

razor slit to the thigh, joy in shame.
No saint, either. Yet might lick

crosses all over this antic, mizzled gloam,
grazing through thought into gospel.

From the Orison, River Stones

White thorn, crimson hips.
Pleasure of the without. Pain of the without.

Venus tucks low here, disappearing
into the mountains' stadia.

What I can't say, stepping into foreign tense
of river, magnetic sluice, arctic tongs,

far-off source without mercy or care for me:
Love has stories not mine to know

or ever tell. Contused fringe, white maiden hair,
lupine, fox ferns, do I project?

Sometimes. I have a rash beneath my shirt,
pubis to lonely breasts. To pass a melancholy hour,

John Clare copied from the *Stamford Mercury*
news of the elderly: old lady by name of Faunt,

who at 105 "has lately cut new teeth,"
a parish clerk, 115, "now able to read without spectacles,

& dig graves." Sad swipe of late middle age,
waters brutishly beautiful & full of flame.

Thus runs the world alway, & we incurable
in its sway. Say it: the world taketh.

But even its farthest reach is ours,
shed cuspid of horizon I pluck up & carry, wet, away.

Reading John Clare, Heading North

Vermont Studio Center

Going alone, with song for company,
homeless at home, homeless at home,
though sometimes time drops from the shoulders,

into hedges with low, darting creeps,
escape-ways, & who are we then.
Skirting the Labour-in-Vain public house,

eating grass to humor hunger.
Getting up as famished as you lay down,
O gipsy, pilgrim in fugue state,

on the lam from Lunacy,
trekking a long way only to be locked away again
"after years of poetical prosing."

Gravel in the shoes recalls the body
to every soul chasing ignis fatuus,
Friar's lantern. *I'll bend down for a dime,*

St Charles Wright said. *I won't for a penny,*
but I will for a dime. In truth, I'm traveling
not on foot, but by air, minute crosshairs

sketching the coast's asphalt amalgam below,
then opening, lowering over green loping
switchbacks capped with ice.

How large a shadow wings must make
caping small things hidden
in another story. A second spring here,

swards in flush, long purples, blue-bottles,
peepers craunking, a red mill shouldering the river,
its small crescent of rapids. Rush and throstle.

"I am in a Mad House & quite forget your name
& who you are," wrote Clare, but also, "I can be miserably happy
in any situation, in any place."

As he was, watching starnels swarm at dusk,
waiting for Death to bring the bill.
Same day, another bed, we're never beyond the right of seizure.

The moon a flipped coin winking in the water's scrawl,
marked with our names though not a word spoken,
riding the sweet black tongue to the falls.

The Wordsworths' Cuckoo Clock

My own thoughts are a wilderness.

—Dorothy Wordsworth

Privy to the sprung year,
this outhouse backyard coliseum

breasts the red wind, cardinals
with their chink of dinnerware,

the wood-pecker's elegant, headstrong
staccato putting antlered horns

on the house, its doorway unhinged
& pillared by a hunted, ankle-hung hare,

an unflinching owl, steep pointed gable
draped with carved oak leaves, acorns,

the whole niche into the philandering psyche
driven by bronze pinecone pendulae, the real pines

free by now of those weights, effusing pollen
without restraint. Way past the marked hour,

the air's still swanked with traffic combers,
a boy crying "here!," & Dorothy writing "tooth broke today

they will soon be gone. Let that pass I shall be
beloved—I want no more," as though, having carried

hoarded mouthfuls all that thirsty way,
she found herself the river.

Dorothy Wordsworth's Doves

A cage is a fletched & ancient harp.
A liar. For though two alabaster,

head-tucked pigeons gargle & thrum
their silhouettes before the window,

at least three hearts mock its regions.
She is attempting a letter today

despite the sieve of her head,
"misty dark & blind." News!

She grapples for tidings as the notched nib
of quill draws up the night,

each cursive scratch a coop to hold
against the aghast, glass shiver,

hung bier, lethal racemes of laburnum
pitching beyond her grasp their skeleton keys.

Temple Sillage

As one who, punished, sweeps
the cell with penitent tongue,

flagstones, straw bits, crumbs fecal,
even the scabbly webs,

hypotenusal in corners, cracks,
each a leprous comb.

Syllables, too, vibrating,
toxic doses that pill,

heave up, rabidly, notes holocaustic
in attar of vertiver, citron, histamine.

Clary sage, I too love
the swallowed creature weight,

prone to dream a dram-
lapped font. The wake of him.

To Time

I know my lover, but who is yours?
Piercing the heart, unbuckling knees,

brining mouth & eyes, gut blinded
by jealous harms? Easy to forget you

in high summer, boys igniting powder,
street-ruckus, fields crackling.

Does it hurt, all those epiphanies
happening beyond you,

the arcane animal stepping out
from woods to white evening road,

body branching into body
like Spanish wine?

Was that beauty or my mind
floating away in a colostrum fletch,

moon's hoodwinked, waxing dream,
youth's lost, decades-fretted face?

I'm not immune to plot or passage.
Are there conversions?

High holiness, ardor growing.
Born, I wore blood on my hands

for many minutes. We drive the arrow.
We do it to you.

Weeping Cherry in Storm

Scoliatic cataract,
already your wet tracts

are second guesses,
milk-glassy, chandeliered,

resembling origin,
history's homeless tiers—

& thieving even rue,
worm that unglues

the pitted heart,
bobeche, in honeyed parts.

I've been borne so many times,
O trial life.

Your spin-drift flakes fall
(that long-ago letter, now in tatters),

& not one in glory.
We are the wind's story.

Exit Wounds

Those Evenings of the Brain
—Emily Dickinson

Horizon pileated with a clock-fattened,
prodigal sun,

long elusive after theaters of rain,
infiltrate my night-gown.

You, too, mercurial cardinals,
brute angels,

& new leaves wealthy with wind
that is your true name.

And when I wake near dawn,
as is my wont,

in pinch of dread, of cobra clutch,
my head bleeding

out into the universe,
& hobble to pee, regain

my see-saw self, you inside me,
then not, show me again my boy

gripping the electric fence,
& the ashen portal out his wrist

where the powers left him safe;
     give me the dead dog's excreta

blooming in the hallway's heat,
     or that perfect trust,

concept of home, shrapnel cells terrorized
     with ancestral want,

a massacre beyond punctuation
     that the alive-again becomes.

Finis Hour

Loaded, lexical, plot's curtain
drops. Crimson. Victorian.

The End. How apply this to the fawn,
struck overnight, now turgid,

a tiny table overturned at road's edge?
The caesurae that bind us

beyond the limits of patter.
What ends in these matters

is not mere words. Vultures disassemble,
verge, then settle.

I drive by. Postpone. Defer.
But closely read dilation, O Fabulator.

The Whales

Belied, be-laired, in sleep's massacred vista
of blood that is the sea within,

like a god, entranced from above,
I felt the whales before I saw them, gorgeous

foetal continents, lost, glistering, parental,
mare-blue beneath sediments of stellar silks,

planktal glass, moving the wrong way
up a narrowing, inland stream.

With all my blindness, I wept
to save them, mysticeti, their kimono lobes,

pharyngeal bells, and lonely spume,
their homesick crying like a scarf of fox grapes

reaching sailors still hundreds of miles
from land. They placental. They

in four-chambered beyonding.
And my own heart, beached—erupting

into hollow room, to closet door,
to clock face, where I failed

and failed again to help them
over the rhapsodic rasures of this world.

From Agitation

Easy, now. The sky cannot have us.
Not yet. What I can never get

enough of is the body,
tongue that tongued my blood

when I. When younger.
Privet hedge, slut of the suburbs,

receive me now, walking, alone,
attar length of an unspent season,

witness to a pair of wrens,
wee ewers carousing the porch

with worsted findings,
nest hidden away, flanking a rogue

thought of mine, unrelayable
as the choked perimeter of prayer.

Celibacy 3

Sleep, why do it? At any glass,
we lip our own mouths.

Rapture when the wind.
Or the waterfall, chalk fenestrations,

small over the dam. Blind plums
swelling all night in a minor key.

Envy of this? Angel of Junipers,
a word to the wise: let's exchange

vows. Or selves.
This is where my mind goes:

why miss night's nada undressing
under dawn's sway?

Call me Bird in the Hand.
Even in windowless rooms, I see sky.

City Lust

Impossible to will surprise,
that particular *other* invading the inside—

patchwork sycamore pushing arms
through rustbelt caries,

anemic rowhouse, medieval remains.
Carnage always in any talk

of awe beyond language:
that Mews in London,

rented hothouse warren,
where, from bed, recovering

from a winter's falsetto spring,
I saw through a lucent file

of back-lot windowpanes
the pristine interiors of three houses,

glimpses into the "litel books"
of minor tragedy, triangulated love

pain converts to fundament,
to act of will, to wild bewilderment.

Barn Owl

In soul I've ever believed,
verdigris, riding sky's gurney,

but the body, the body I made up,
keyhole I peered through,

until. . . . But that tale belongs
to love. What owner of this

asymmetric knifing of night,
famished flesh-clef, ruthless shriek

announcing the about-to-be-finished
minute, whatever, scuttling below,

already registered & processed
by satellite dish skull, cochlear miracle,

evolution's cruel heart-face?
Never, even in pelvic dilation, crowning,

another universe boring through me,
cowled, vernix-blind, came such noise

as this. What somber mote now rises,
its moment demolished, un-mined?

Accidental

Broken mantle clock, squat turreted castle
kept for its hand-painted closet,

coiled beehive in gauzy umlaut of wings,
gilding pale as the heat the vagina gives off,

after—. After what? An afterthought, now,
to change "vagina," for modesty's sake,

to "portal to this world." Truth is, the key
signature of any day's measure can be altered

of a wild sudden. How a deleted "i"
turns another word to "marred," for instance.

Bond indifferent as a dish of untouched soaps.
Shaped like eggs, no less. What is it

floods our clothes in the muddled dusk
of our beginnings? Is it what's inside the door

of the flawed clock, a fury of shadows
cast by nothing? Fluke or fate,

whatever happens or doesn't happen,
the portal happened once. To make you,

you who were an I. To make me,
the child you were. You what I will be.

The Wind Wears a Red Leaf

Catherine wheels, star-pox, wedding gem,
Libra's fulcrum & scoured pans,

pyrotechnics hid by rain drilling the night
I woke & woke in another room,

hands sour from your last changing.
Did it move in the brain, what ranges

incarnate, then departs, Dementia the cat
astray at the ankles, then at the door,

vapor spark-rocket, Bede's brief sparrow,
branch from Newton's apple tree

a cosmos away in satellite space station,
allowed at last to cross the heavens

plural and jealous after all these years?
Mother-May-I? Or does it travel

to frozen north, alcoholic,
collapse in slippage, mortal aorta,

where coats are turning inside out
& can't admit or fathom spirit?

Silver torch of your birth name, Kay—
Where is it now that you are sky?

Temple Tomb

John 20: 11–18

In this marrow season,
trunks tarnished, paused,

I am garden. Am before.
Asleep. Then the changes:

placental, myrrhed. Wet hem
when you appeared.

What did your body ever have
to do with me? In my astonished mouth,

enskulled jawbone guessed,
though as yet I didn't know you.

You sprung. You now intransitive,
tense with heaven.

Gardener, which of us said do not touch.
Which one of us was undressed?

White Deer

Have I fed too long on myth,
your quicksilver canthus shims,

vanquished pearl flank
in fractured scrim at day's close,

limning the charcoal grapevine
wicker, shy, blood-licked?

And lived as much in your satin,
eroding shoal, elusive beyond garrison

fencing, caparisoned woods,
myrrh of squirrel, streaming traffic coals,

as I do here, in room-trapped
shadows run amok, menace

of bedstead, window sill, chair's lap?
If a truly cloistered nun, I might, to bind

gold-leaf to parchment
and—to touch—your topaz horns,

grind chalk on porphyry slab,
add mastic & just a shop-cat's lick

of cream, checking its sweetness
with my own mouthed brush,

before applying the orient sadness,
odd ebullience in this chaste text.

Morel Patch

Ghetto miraculous,
   tipsy monastery, mysterious

embroidery erupting rashly
   in thatch beneath the dying ash,

gnomic roofs of steep snows,
   bee skeps on hollow stems, blown

honeycombed tutulus
   with whiff of kiosk,

cloister, old world side-show
   trousered intimacy, glass-blowers,

or the throat swollen in filigree
   by a swallowed key, or bee:

intoxication, bell whose knell
   or tonic only time can tell.

St. Field

You months gone, I lift the curtain
thumb-tacked over shelf boards,

jelly glasses shellacked with dust,
decades-old cataracts of paraffin,

glaucous, into the back field,
skin miasmic, wild strawberries,

a dead bird there once, underneath,
weasand eye full of sky.

In fall, files of quail, the world
in subtraction as menarchal

fox grapes filled the same pot
that in winter scalded fletch and fur

from pheasants, rabbits, another oil
in the mouth. Chassis of a dumped car

where we played, witchgrass, sumac
pushing through floorboards, door-less,

the glove compartment mice-infested.
Cigarette trays, resinous with rain,

cannabis. Decay of sugar maples
curdling the jaw, corms buried

in pelvic registers, like your voice
even now rending me over it.

My Father's Dream of Thoreau

What shall I learn of beans or beans of me?
Henry David Thoreau, *Walden*

He doesn't know it, but he's in the long row
with Thoreau, decades behind him, boyish soul

in old body bent over an ancient tool,
Johnson grass & crab already whispering *fool, fool,*

claiming, impatient, the mile he's just hoed,
craven moon above glistered as the needle's eye

his dead wife mouths, whiskery tail of thread,
linsey-woolsey stitching of bean plants moth-eaten by deer

that step behind him, soundless, this time a doe
and two new fawns in voracious flow,

tracks labial in the fresh chop. Why do it, then,
so much more than he can ever salvage, eat, or share,

well past eighty, though the holes he makes, in cindered din,
are not for himself to lie down in. A catch of rain

hums farewell in a notched gauge; netted by stars,
wasp-gouged pears drop, surreptitious,

a visitor's foot-fall coming from the orchard
whether he's ready, or not. How then can our harvest fail,

Henry calls back to him, cheery, hale,
in the nineteenth-century voice

of his father's father, also a farmer, when a furrow
has never cared one whit for its husband?

Once in A

Why blue? Why *blue* moon,
   lagniappe lens
drilling the blinds?

Like the multiple orgasm
   in which some never
will believe, the lexicon

yields up a trove
   of speculation, tracing
the hue of the big O,

coming more than once
   a month, to atmosphere,
an accident of ions and the eye,

like the sky, the argent
   ridge of mountains.
But ponder the Old English

cognate, *belewe*,
   "to betray":
double-crossing old saints—

loneliness, love, the calendar—
   tricking night into day
as though there will always be another.

Ignis Fatuus

A dove's-neck sky banks sulphur maples,
    burns quince, townhouse fires
(still, *real* fires), & the pelvis

clenches, quavery, as since childhood,
    in gunning season, weird exhilaration
hidden on cellar stairs, men below in caps

circling boiling pots, red water,
    gripping tendoned claws, guttering,
guns at rest, disjointed and oiled,

pheasants, a rabbit's long paws,
    smoke & scraped down, newspaper,
blooded jacket pockets, portent

of a later privacy, rank pad
    of the soughed, fertile self.
And then, after more years,

not. Beauty on the block.
    Ordure recoiling girl into landscape,
her own death. December

just over the blue ridge. Tune
    of a foolish fire blown
into the unlikely pipe of a vulture bone.

Reading an Old Book

Inside is a yolked tulip
   clad with snow,
toluene, benzaldehyde,

almond sleet, vanillin,
   a ragged span,
like the seagull blown inland

by dented sky, storm,
   my father a widower
one week, stalled by its bluster,

blizzard pages rappelling
   toward the windshield & back,
something leaking through

the traffic, the roundabout,
   his scientist's doubt,
deciphering now a "w,"

now an "m," then away
   in mackled breakdown
of sky, lignin, he might say,

releasing chemicals, nostalgia—no,
   admit it, the neural mesh of being,
the yielding vehicle that lets him go.

The Holidays

As my eyes can seem to me one,
but are of course two, I am not you,

in crux of a plane now passing over
apricot canyons, falls, clouds

hurled through by hummingbirds
in cardiac, migratory throngs, or water vapor

becoming its farthest extent, icicle
one can suck the edges of, a glacial glove.

Love, the fume of this fir tree,
bucketed and hauled indoors,

is distance visible, a phantom North,
exhaling roots it once had, webs,

birds it held, this glass swallow
with faux tail-feather I clip to a branch,

fingers knuckle-deep in balsam prickle,
then into boxed tissue, orbs unburied,

dangling their "S" crooks of wire.
I hang the ceramic owl, wooden gull,

on the window side, spin them
in light's brazier: your thumb

at my lips, *hush, hush.*
It's just a host of mirroring globes

ghosting the face, as any stasis
offends desire, a peering

into uncoaxed sky, mussel-blue
& not unlike a god, dead set against repose.

Duet

New Year's Eve

Two sisters side by side,
benched at the gleaming fin

of the living room's out-of-tune baby grand,
work out a mash-up, Adele's "Hello"

& Kate Bush's "Wuthering Heights,"
Hello, it's me. . ., Heathcliff, it's me, it's Cathy,

voices by turns treble, then cemetery-dusked,
meandering, & hungry

as the sinew-tracks of moles
sponging December's yard,

painted mouths of iced puddles,
branchless leaves snaring the window

with inhuman gale.
One swallows this heavy beauty,

rolls the mordent perfume
back to bloom as the other slips out

of autumn's whalebone stave, descant.
They sing as if still girls. As if before

love's scarlet evidence, & not, like the year,
the trees, already moved, moved through.

Temple On My Knees

When this day returns to me
I will value your heart,
long hurt in long division,
over mine. Mouth above mine too—
say you love me, truth never more
meant, *say you are angry.*
Words, words we net with our mouths.
Soul is an old thirst but not as first
as the body's perhaps,
though on bad nights its melancholy
eats us out, to a person.
True, time is undigressing.
Yet true is all we can be:
rhyming you, rhyming me.

How I Might Sound if I Left Myself Alone

Turning to watch you leave,
I see we must always walk toward

other rooms, river of heaven
between two office buildings.

Orphaned cloud, cioppino poppling,
book spined in the open palm. Unstoppable light.

I think it is all right.
Or do tonight, garden toad

a speaking stone,
young sound in an old heart.

Annul the self? I float it,
a day lily in my wine. Oblivion?

I love our lives,
keeping me from it.

NOTES

"Temple Moon" is for Ron Slate.

"Snowdrops" is for Claudia Emerson (1957–2014).

"A Labour of" is a term of "venery," an archaic word for hunting—many of them found in *The Book of Saint Alban's* (1486)—including such phrases as a "murder of crows," "pride of lions," and an "exaltation of larks."

"Wandering Womb" speaks back to the ancient notion, prevailing into the early modern era, that the womb could "wander" throughout the female body, causing any number of medical pathologies, including hysteria.

"Abridged Hour," "Hour Bleu-aille," and *"Finis* Hour" owe to Maggie Nelson's *Bluets* and Garrett Stewart's *Death Sentences*.

"Temple Serein" evokes a rain that falls, usually at dusk, from a cloudless ("serene") sky.

"Reading John Clare, Heading North" is for Stephen Margulies

"Temple Sillage" concerns, in part, the degree to which a scent or perfume lingers after its source has passed.

"The Wordsworths's Cuckoo Clock" and "Dorothy Wordsworth's Doves" refer tangentially to the twenty-some years of dementia suffered by Dorothy Wordsworth, who, before her mind deteriorated in her 60s, kept journals of exquisite and perceptive prose.

"The Wind Wears a Red Leaf": In 2010, a piece of the apple tree that helped Sir Isaac Newton explain principals of gravity and the laws of motion was launched into space aboard the shuttle Atlantis toward the International Space Station. "The Wind Wears a Red Leaf" and "Accidental" are in memoriam, Kay Smith Russ, 1935–2014.

"Temple Tomb" reimagines events depicted in John 20: 11–18.

"Morel Patch" is for APS.

"My Father's Dream of Thoreau" contains two phrases from Thoreau's chapter "The Bean-Field" in *Walden*: "not for himself to lie down in" and "how then can our harvest fail."

"Reading an Old Book": The breakdown of certain chemicals used in paper and binding materials causes antique volumes to emit a distinctive aroma of vanilla and almonds.

"Duet" is for JAS and SRS.

ACKNOWLEDGMENTS

Grateful acknowledgment is made to the editors of the following journals, in which the poems named below first appeared or are forthcoming, occasionally in a now altered version or with a different title:

Bear Review: "A Labour of"
Blackbird: "Accidental" "The Wind Wears a Red Leaf"
Boston Review: "Ice Idyll"
Connotation Press: "Scarlet Tanager"
The Cortland Review: "Worry Yoga"
Hampden-Sydney Review: "Weeping Cherry in Storm"
Image: Art, Faith, Mystery: "Furta Sacra" "Temple Gaudete" "Temple Tomb"
Jai-Alai #2: "Orexic Hour" "To Time"
Missouri Review (on-line): "Owl Hour" "Snowdrops"
The Plume Poetry Anthology 2014: "Mynddaeg Hour"
The Plume Poetry Anthology 2016: "White Deer"
Plume (on-line): "Abridged Hour" "*Finis* Hour" "Hour Bleu-aille"
Poetry: "How I Might Sound if I Left Myself Alone" "Temple on My Knees" "Temple You"
Quarterly West: "Baroque Hour"
Shenandoah: "From the Orison, River Stones"
Smartish Pace: "Temple Serein" "Temple Sillage" "Wandering Womb"
Southwest Review: "Friday Night Hour"
Streetlight: "Temple Age"
Thoreau Society Bulletin: "My Father's Dream of Thoreau"
TUBA: "Temple Solstice" "Temple Surrender"
Virginia Quarterly Review: "Celibacy 1" "Celibacy 2"
Wave Composition: "City Lust" "Reading an Old Book" "The Whales"
Waxwing: "From Agitation" "Plum Hour"

"Temple Gaudete" was reprinted in the *Pushcart Prize Anthology* (2016) (40th Anniversary Edition)
"Furta Sacra" was reprinted at *Poetry Daily* (7 September 2014)
"St. Field" appears in *The Echoing Green: Poems of Fields, Meadows, and Grasses* (Knopf / Everyman's Pocket Poetry Series, April 2016)

I thank the Vermont Studio Center for the gift of two Visiting Writer Residencies, which afforded time and space for composing and compiling these poems. Several of these poems were begun during a Guggenheim Fellowship year, a spell for which I remain grateful. My abiding gratitude to Carole Weinstein and, as ever, to my editor, Gabriel Fried, and to Karen and Michael Braziller and all of the Persea family.

ABOUT THE AUTHOR

Lisa Russ Spaar is the author of five books of poetry, including *Glass Town, Blue Venus, Satin Cash,* and *Vanitas, Rough*; and a collection of essays, *The Hide-and-Seek Muse: Annotations of Contemporary Poetry.* She is also the editor of the anthologies *Acquainted with the Night: Insomnia Poems, All that Mighty Heart: London Poems,* and *Monticello in Mind: Fifty Contemporary Poems on Jefferson.* Her poems have appeared in *Poetry, Boston Review, IMAGE, Virginia Quarterly Review,* and many other journals and quarterlies, as well as in the *Best American Poetry* and *Pushcart Prize Anthology* series.

Spaar's honors include a Guggenheim Fellowship, a Rona Jaffe Award, the Carole Weinstein Poetry Prize for Poetry, an Outstanding Faculty Award from the State Council of Higher Education for Virginia, the Library of Virginia Award for Poetry, a Virginia Foundation for the Humanities fellowship, and the 2013–2014 Faculty Award of the Jefferson Scholars Foundation. A 2014 Finalist for the National Book Circle Critics Award for Excellence in Reviewing, her commentaries and columns about poetry appear regularly in *The Chronicle of Higher Education,* the *Washington Post,* the *New York Times,* the *Los Angeles Review of Books,* and elsewhere. She is currently Horace W. Goldsmith NEH Distinguished Teaching Professor at the University of Virginia, where she is Professor of English and Creative Writing.